℗ CHILDRENS PRESS   1224 West Van Buren Street, Chicago, Illinois 60607

MANIA BOOKS

START A READING MANIA with THE MA̶ ̶
about high-interest subject̶
have created a new s̶

Baseball Mania

By Ed and Ruth Radlauer

AN ELK GROVE BOOK

 CHILDRENS PRESS, CHICAGO

Photo credits:
    Los Angeles Dodgers Baseball Club, Cover, pages, 4–9, 21–29, 31

Library of Congress Cataloging in Publication Data

Radlauer, Edward.
  Baseball mania.
  (Mania books)
  ''An Elk Grove book.''
  SUMMARY: An easy-to-read introduction to the game of
baseball.
    1. Baseball—Juvenile literature. [1. Baseball]
I. Radlauer, Ruth Shaw, joint author. II. Title.
GV867.5.R32   796.357   80-12295
ISBN 0-516-07778-3

1 2 3 4 5 6 7 8 9 10 11 12 13 14 15 R 86 85 84 83 82 81 80

A RADLAUER

Mania Book

CREATED FOR CHILDRENS PRESS BY
*RADLAUER PRODUCTIONS INCORPORATED

Baseball mania?

Yes, this is baseball mania.
It's time to "Play ball!"

Sometimes you are
the pitcher.

And sometimes you
are the batter.

You may be a catcher—

—or play in the field.

Some people like softball.

In softball you
pitch underhand.

11

If you hit
the underhand pitch—

—a fielder will try
to stop it.

If you swing and miss—

—that's a strike. Three
strikes and you're out.

Go to the dugout.

You stay in the dugout
until it's time to play
or bat again.

A baseball coach—

—can help you be
a better player.

The coach shows you how
to run the bases—

—and how to slide.

If you slide,
the umpire watches.

The umpire watches to
call you safe or out.

Baseball players need
lots of practice.

Practice makes you
a better player.

Yes, sometimes you
play baseball—

—and sometimes you
talk baseball.
Talk baseball?

Baseball is a
good day game—

—or night game.

But day or night—

—it's baseball mania.

31

Baseball words

Page

4   baseball, mania
5   yes, this, is, it's, time, to, play, ball
6   sometimes, you, are, the, pitcher
7   and, batter
8   may, be, a, catcher
9   or, in, field
10   some, people, like, softball
11   pitch, underhand
12   if, hit
13   fielder, will, try, stop, it
14.   swing, miss
15   that's, strike, three, strikes, you're, out
16   go, dugout
17   stay, until, bat, again
18   coach
19   can, help, better, player
20   shows, how, run, bases
21   slide
22   umpire, watches
23   call, safe
24   players, need, lots, of, practice
25   makes
26
27   talk
28   good, day, game
29   night
30   but
31